Not Ae

Diane Lindsey Reeves

Ferguson
An imprint of Infobase Publishing

Acknowledgements

Special thanks to Anna Carter, Mark Sanderson, Chris Schaefer,
and Luke Snyder for sharing stories about their interesting work,
and to Lacey Reeves for sharing her ideas and inspiration.
A huge thank you to Joy Strickland and Catherine Davis
who assisted in researching and writing this book.

Way Out Work: Freaky Jobs

Copyright © 2009 by Diane Lindsey Reeves

Ferguson
An imprint of Infobase Publishing
132 West 31st Street
New York NY 10001

Library of Congress Cataloging-in-Publication Data

Reeves, Diane Lindsey, 1959-
  Freaky jobs / Diane Lindsey Reeves.—1st ed.
      p. cm.—(Way out work)
  Includes index.
  ISBN-13: 978-1-60413-132-1 (hardcover : alk. paper)
  ISBN-10: 1-60413-132-2 (hardcover : alk. paper) 1. Occupations. 2. Professions. I. Title.
  HB2581.R45 2009
  331.702—dc22

                              2009005771

Ferguson books are available at special discounts when purchased in bulk quantities for businesses, associations, institutions, or sales promotions. Please call our Special Sales Department in New York at (212) 967-8800 or (800) 322-8755.

You can find Ferguson on the World Wide Web at http://www.fergpubco.com

Text design by Erika K. Arroyo
Cover design by Jooyoung An

Printed in the United States of America

Bang MSRF 10 9 8 7 6 5 4 3 2 1

This book is printed on acid-free paper.

Contents

Introduction

There's *freaky* as in way-out weird. And there's *freaky* as in way-out wow. This book introduces how people work their way into both kinds of freaky jobs. Although these types of jobs range from bizarre food chef to circus performer, the one thing they all have in common is that they are never boring.

Whether it's cracking super codes or cloning human genes, there really isn't a typical day at the office for people who have freaky jobs. Some are so fast paced—like racecar mechanics and rodeo riders—that you'll have to rev up your engines or saddle up your horses just to keep up with them.

If you're looking for an out-of-the-ordinary way to make a living, you've come to the right place. Here's where you'll find profiles introducing several freaky jobs and encounter interesting features sure to get you thinking in new and unexpected ways. Then take a quick look at more freaky job ideas and stop by to read about some people doing some rather unusual work. Make sure to spend a little time exploring the end of the book, where you can play around with some activities and find out once and for all if a freaky job is right for you.

Bizarre Food Chef

A cook dresses up a plate of deep-fried worms served with a dollop of guacamole. *AP Photo/ Daro Lopez-Mills*

What's for dinner? How about some hot and spicy chicken feet topped with a side of fried scorpion? No? Maybe you'd prefer some grilled octopus served up with some stinky tofu? Clean your plate, or else there's no ox tongue ice cream for dessert. Sound good? Believe it or not, these dishes are considered delicacies in some cultures and, in some cases, are gaining popularity in upscale restaurants in some of the more "cosmopolitan" locales in the United States.

Television shows like Travel Channel's *Bizarre Foods* are feeding this trend. The show, hosted by famous food writer and chef Andrew Zimmern, features his globetrotting adventures in search of the world's weirdest food. So far his travels have taken him to places like the Louisiana bayou, where large water rodents comprised the main dish, the Amazon, where fresh piranha was the catch of the day, and Malaysia, where it was bat meat on the menu.

Other bizarre food chefs stick closer to home and tend to work in restaurants catering to adventurous eaters. While they may not travel as much as Zimmern, they are still influenced by the various flavors of the world and look for inventive ways to concoct new taste sensations.

In fact, you might say that bizarre food chefs are "culinary historians." They use food to understand other places and peoples. A community that regularly sautés worms differs greatly from one that eats pizza and French fries, after all. Looking at the food can tell these chefs about the environment of the region (people who eat

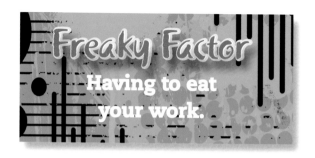

eels more likely than not live near the ocean) and about the lifestyle of the people. Some bizarre food experts also use food as research, writing books about the meals just like historians write books about wars and politics.

And, by the way, weird food isn't the only freaky thing you're likely to find in restaurant kitchens these days. Many chefs are using technology in decidedly unusual ways to cook up some interesting new edible innovations. Part scientist, part technology geek, and part chef, these "molecular

According to Charles Sell, an organic chemist who specializes in producing flavors and fragrances for Givaudan, the secret to recreating the smell of strawberries involves mixing the burnt-sugar aroma of candyfloss with the bouquet of fresh-cut grass and adding a whiff of...vomit.

What Do You Think?

In some Middle Eastern and Asian cultures, burping after a good meal is considered a compliment to the chef. Yet in our culture it would be considered extremely rude. How is it possible that the very same action is viewed in two completely different ways?

gastronomists" are shaking things up in kitchens and laboratories around the world. Some call it kitchen

GO FOR IT IF. . .

You like to try all different kinds of food.

- - - - - - - - - - - - - - - -

You're a picky eater.

FORGET ABOUT IT IF. . .

chemistry while others refer to it as the science of deliciousness, but all agree that the end result is often rather tasty. For instance, did you know that if you very carefully add a bit of liquid nitrogen to your favorite homemade ice cream ingredients it will freeze almost instantly? A new fast-food favorite!

About the only thing you can say when it comes to these new food trends is this: One person's *yucky* is another person's *yummy*. Of course, for those with stomachs of steel and hyperactive taste buds, they also offer some interesting ways to cook up an interesting career.

Go Online to Find Out More!
Explore the world of food and nutrition at http://www. nutritionexplorations.org.

Circus Performer

Surrounded by a ring of fire, contortionist Serchmaa Byamba performs in "The Fire Odyssey," an adaptation of Homer's *Odyssey*. *AP Photo/Noah Berger*

"Ladies and gentlemen, children of all ages..." Those words, uttered in a big, booming voice by a ringmaster attired in a bright red coat and tall black top hat, mean just one thing: The circus has come to town! Since the late 1700s, audiences everywhere have enjoyed a three-ring extravaganza of clowns, trapeze artists, lions, elephants, and so much more.

As much fun as it is to watch a circus, can you imagine how much fun it might be to work in one? Make no mistake—this is not your typical day

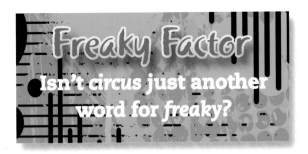

job. Circus performers are remarkably talented people who travel around the world enthralling audiences with their daring deeds and death-defying stunts.

One of the most popular acts is the flying trapeze. To get an idea of what a trapeze artist does, imagine doing an Olympics-worthy gymnastics routine at, say, 30 feet off the ground. Take this imaginary scene one step farther by picturing what it would be like to do an elaborate balance beam routine on a rope strung high above a roaring crowd in a huge circus tent. Got the picture? Now, think about what it would be like to do the routine all over again on a unicycle. That's what a tightrope walker does. Watch out— that first step can be a doozy!

Acrobats are another popular circus act—all the more because they make what they do look so easy. If you want to call standing on your head on top of an elephant's back

What Do You Think?

P. T. Barnum, one of the world's most famous ringmasters and the creator of "the greatest show on earth," was known to say, "There's a sucker born every minute." What do you suppose he meant?

WOW!

What began in the 1980s as the High Heels Club, a festival for stilt walkers, turned into a reinvention of what the 21st-century circus is all about. Now known around the world as Cirque du Soleil ("circus of the sun" in French), these performers mix circus acts with original music, special effects, and spectacular costumes. Check out their Web site at http://www.cirquedusoleil.com.

GO FOR IT IF. . .

You'd do anything for a
laugh or the sound
of applause.

- - - - - - - - - - - - - -

You'd rather stick close to
home than hang out in a
three-ring circus tent.

FORGET ABOUT IT IF. . .

easy, go ahead. But you probably don't want to try that trick at home! Acrobats are famous for performing amazing stunts on moving objects— animals, rolling balls, and even other acrobats.

But, have no fear (of heights!); some types of circus performers never leave the ground. They just do things like put their heads in lion's mouths, juggle with sharp knives, and swallow fire. After all that, it's probably a relief to see the clowns come zipping through in their tiny cars. They seem almost normal clowning around and yukking it up with the crowd, in spite of their outrageous costumes and ridiculous antics.

As you may have already concluded for yourself, circus performers tend to be talented, strong, physically fit, and very committed to doing what they do with precision and panache. It's not for everyone, though, and especially not for people who prefer the comforts of home. Circus performers travel from one location to another, pitching their tents, perfecting their acts, and bringing out the "kid" in audiences of all ages.

Go Online to Find Out More!

You don't have to run away to join this circus; just go online to the Ringling Bros. and Barnum & Bailey "fun zone" at http://www. ringling.com.

Cryptologist

Paul Kocher displays a World War II–era Enigma cipher machine at the annual RSA Conference in San Francisco in 2007. *Paul Chinn/San Francisco Chronicle/Corbis*

What is a cryptologist? Shhh...It's a secret.

But wait a minute. Maybe you can figure this out for yourself. If cryptology is the study of secret communication, what do you think a cryptologist does? If you guessed something like, "They are people who write and crack secret codes," you are on the right track. These days, cryptologists are highly skilled in things like mathematics and computer science and are more likely than most people to spend their free time as musicians or chess masters (activities that also require analytic and deciphering skills).

At this point you may be wondering, "What's with all the secrets, and why would anyone need to crack them?" Businesses use cryptologists to keep important information about their products and plans away from the prying eyes of their competitors. Banks use them to protect their customers' money. Cryptology is especially popular among governments and military forces that use secret codes to protect sensitive information and work really hard to break the secret codes of other governments and military forces. This can be especially important in a time of war, when keeping enemies guessing can mean the difference between victory and defeat.

In fact, one of the most well-known stories about cryptology occurred during World War II. More than 400 Navajo Native Americans were eventually recruited by

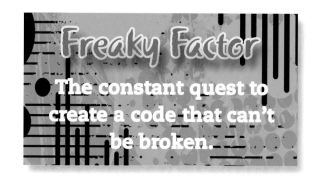

the United States Marines to convey secret messages between each other in their native language. Since Navajo is such a difficult and specialized language, military leaders felt reasonably certain that none of their Axis enemies—the Germans, Italians, and Japanese—would be able to understand these messages. According to historical records, they were right. In one instance, Navajo "codetalkers" sent more than 800 messages during the pivotal battle of Iwo Jima and none of them were cracked by the enemy.

WOW!

Did you know that your parent probably carries around an encrypted, super-secret code in his or her wallet? Yep. It's called an ATM card and it involves some very complicated technology that helps keep their money safe.

Besides using obscure languages, cryptologists use a variety of increasingly sophisticated techniques to send and intercept secret messages. At the simplest level, cryptologists use codes, or systems of symbols or signals, in ways that have evolved since ancient times, when people scrambled letters or replaced them with numbers to hide sensitive information. Today, cryptologists use high-tech mathematics, including algorithms (fancy problem-solving formulas) to disguise what needs to be said. Of course, computers have added new dimensions of both complexity and ease to the business of making and breaking secret codes. Super-powerful computers are used to create codes so complex that it could take an outsider years to break them. Computers also help with the complex calculations so that cryptographers don't have to spend endless hours figuring them out by hand.

What Do You Think?

When Julius Caesar, a ruler of the ancient Roman Empire, needed to send a secret message, he shifted each letter by three. So the letter "A" was replaced with the letter "D," the letter "B" with the letter "E," and so on. Can you use this ancient code to create a message of your own?

GO FOR IT IF. . .

Solving puzzles is among your favorite pastimes.

- - - - - - - - - - - - - - - - - -

You can't keep a secret.

FORGET ABOUT IT IF. . .

Go Online to Find Out More!

Become a cryptologist at http://www.nsa.gov/KIDS.

Genetic Engineer

Have you ever wished you could change the texture of your hair or the shape of your eyes? Have you ever wished you were smarter, stronger, or better at sports? Have you ever had so much to do that you wished there was another you to help? Someday you may get these wishes and more—thanks to new discoveries in genetic engineering!

Genetic engineers are scientists who alter the structure of DNA in a living organism. DNA is short for deoxyribonucleic acid, and it is the stuff found in virtually every cell in your body that makes you who you are.

Until fairly recently, DNA was a mystery that baffled humans. Three

A genetic engineer and his medical technical lab assistant prepare samples in a laboratory. *Waltraud Grubitzsch/dpa/Landov*

What Do You Think?

In 1997, scientific history was made when the first fully cloned mammal was born. The result, a lamb named Dolly, lived until 2003 and gave birth to six lambs of her own. What do you think are the benefits and problems that cloning might bring?

scientists who eventually figured out the structure of DNA—Francis Crick, James Watson, and Maurice Wilkins— not only won the Nobel Prize for medicine in 1962, but also are credited with making the most important biological discovery of the past 100 years. Some would also say they opened a new frontier of science exploration that would be significant for at least 100 years more.

Because of their discovery and others that followed, genetic engineers can now splice, chop, manipulate, and switch DNA bits in ways that change certain aspects of living things. At first, some of these changes may seem insignificant. For instance, some genetic work has focused on making plants resistant to a certain type of beetle and creating cows with thicker hair. "So what?" you may wonder. However, even changes like these can make the world a better place. For instance, a plant that is resistant to bugs survives longer, which gives it more time to grow food to feed hungry people. And those hairy cows? They can be bred in cold regions where plants don't grow and provide a source of food and money to people living there.

Of course, the potential promise of DNA gets even more powerful. Engineers expect that in addition to improving food sources (like the plant and the cow), they may someday be able to manipulate genes that could result in major breakthroughs in health and medicine. For example, if scientists can identify what type of DNA causes dyslexia (the mixing-up of letters which makes reading and writing difficult for some people), then they can fix the problem and help kids

WOW!

DNA is a double helix and, when magnified under a microscope, looks like a twisted ladder.

GO FOR IT IF...

You can't wait for science class!

White lab coats are the last thing you want to put on.

FORGET ABOUT IT IF...

read better. Some genetic engineers hope to manipulate DNA to cure cancer and other life-threatening diseases. Developments like these could actually increase the length and quality of millions of lives.

The idea that scientists could someday clone humans was once the stuff of far-fetched science fiction movies. Recent breakthroughs in genetics have made that idea a little more possible. The ethical use of this new knowledge is a subject of heated debate among scientists and politicians alike.

Besides taking this responsibility very seriously, future geneticists must become experts in subjects like biol-

ogy, chemistry, and math. Gaining all of this knowledge generally begins in high school and extends through college and beyond. Genetic engineers spend years studying and earning advanced degrees.

All of those hours pay off, though, because genetic engineers get to work on the cutting edge of science, using some of the world's most sophisticated technology.

One of the most important projects is called the Human Genome Project, which began in 1990. Genetic engineers are working hard to map the DNA of humans and other organisms, locating each gene and identifying its structure and function. So far they have mapped human DNA, but they are still busy trying to figure out the function for a high percentage of it.

Go Online to Find Out More!
Become an expert on genetics and cloning at http://www.uidaho.edu/ clonezone.

Pet Psychologist

A pet psychologist examines a bulldog in her office. *Larry Williams/zefa/Corbis*

Did you know that bad behavior is the number one cause of death for household pets like cats and dogs? It's not that these animals die in the course of their misdeeds; but rather because of them. What happens is that their misbehavior becomes so unmanageable that their owners release them to animal shelters, where somewhere between and 5 and 10 million dogs and cats are "put down" each year.

Behaviors likely to doom pets include acting aggressively (biting people or fighting with other animals), destroying property with excessive scratching or chewing, and doing their "business" inside the house instead of outside. Some even suffer from fear and anxiety-based conditions (typically related to noise, social or separation anxiety, or other stressors) that make them difficult to

17

deal with. Others actually become depressed, and it's tied to many of the same causes as in humans: grief from the loss of a loved one, boredom, or chemical imbalance. Dogs that constantly bark at nothing, dig holes in the backyard, chase their tails, or destroy property may actually be afflicted with an obsessive-compulsive disorder (OCD). Note the key word "constantly." Most dogs exhibit these behaviors some of the time, but dogs with OCD do them so often that, frankly, it can drive their human caregivers (and the neighbors!) nuts.

But here's the good news: These problems can generally be solved without resorting to the rather drastic measure of euthanizing annoying pets. So how do pet psychologists "treat" their four-legged patients? It's not like they can have the animals lie on a couch and talk about what's bothering them, right? Of course not, although you are welcome to try! Instead, pet psychologists rely mostly on two types of treatment that are also commonly used with humans: behavior modification and medication. Behavior modification generally involves training (or retraining) a pet to respond differently to certain kinds of stimuli. It involves redirecting misbehavior with more positive actions and, perhaps most important of all, training its owners to deal with the behavior more effectively.

For instance, a pet psychologist might recommend that an owner swaddle a pet who gets stressed out

WOW!

The American Pet Product Manufacturers Association reports that Americans spend more than an estimated $40 billion on pets each year.

What Do You Think?

What are some ways that people could learn to enjoy their pets more so that fewer animals are put to sleep in animal shelters?

during thunderstorms in a body wrap in much the same way that a parent would swaddle a crying newborn. This technique often proves useful in calming sensory nerves and helping pets—and babies—feel more secure. In situations in which dogs misbe-

have when owners are gone for long periods of time, arranging "doggy daycare" or regular play dates with other pets makes for happier, better-behaved animal companions.

Of course, just like in humans, sometimes the problems are due to physical problems or chemical imbalances. In those cases, pet psychologists rely on a wide variety of natural and pharmaceutical remedies to get the pet feeling (and acting) better.

Another name for a pet psychologist is an animal behaviorist. These well-trained professionals tend to work in pet hospitals, at veterinary schools, or in private practices that blend treatment and training.

GO FOR IT IF. . .

You are a problem-solving animal lover.

- - - - - - - - - - - - - -

You are allergic to animals—achoo!

FORGET ABOUT IT IF. . .

Go Online to Find Out More!

Bone up on your knowledge about different breeds of cats, dogs, and horses at http://www. terrificpets.com.

Racecar Mechanic

Mechanics of Scuderia Ferrari inspect a Formula One race car. *Gero Breloer/dpa/Landov*

the maximum highway speed of 75 miles per hour!), the racecars go round and round, sometimes lapping the track hundreds of times before the competition is over. With hours of high-speed driving ahead of them, as is the case in races like the famous Indy 500, racecar drivers depend on elite, highly skilled teams

What Do You Think?
The typical racecar isn't your granny's car. But there are some similarities, and automakers often look to resourceful racecar mechanics for innovations. Come up with a list of ideas and then go online to the How Stuff Works Web site (http://auto. howstuffworks.com/top-10-car-tech-from-racing.htm) to compare lists.

"Ladies and gentlemen, start your engines…" With those famous words and the sight of an official waving two green flags, racecar drivers take off down the track.

Reaching speeds in excess of 230 miles per hour (compared with

of mechanics to get them to the finish line.

During races, these teams, called pit crews, have to move, move, move, fast, fast, fast to keep their teams' cars in the race. To get an idea of just how fast they have to move, set a timer for 14 seconds. From the time you push start to the time you hear the buzzer ring, a pit crew would have changed four tires, filled the tank with over 100 pounds of gas (that's about 18 gallons), and made any necessary repairs. How do they do it?

In a word: teamwork! A typical team consists of a rear tire carrier and a rear tire changer as well as a front tire carrier and front tire changer. You can probably guess what their responsibilities are, can't you? To change the tires! Then there's the jackman, who operates a hydraulic jack to raise the car so the tires can be changed—first the right side, then the left. The gas man fills the tank with fuel with assistance from the catch can man, who catches any overflowing fuel in a can (hence the name, *catch can man*!) and signals the team to let them know when the car has been refueled. There's also a support crew outside the pit helping out by providing supplies and tools. In some cases, an extra man is allowed in the pit to clean the windshield and check on the driver.

Of course, long before a race ever begins, these and other specially trained mechanics have been hard at work building, maintaining, fine-tuning, and repairing these

WOW!

Did you know that a racecar traveling at 220 miles per hour can travel the length of a football field in about a second?

GO FOR IT IF. . .

You have an insatiable need for speed!

– – – – – – – – – – – – – –

Cars just aren't your thing. What's the difference between a VW and a BMW, anyway?

FORGET ABOUT IT IF. . .

"lean, mean racing machines." Keeping a racecar in winning condition involves constant attention to every detail and creative use of state-of-the-art technologies. This means, of course, that racecar mechanics have to be a step above the average mechanic entrusted with your family car.

Racecar mechanics have to know more than what's under the hood of the cars they work on. They rely on a sound understanding of racing theory, from speed variations to tire inflation, and they even go so far as applying physics and high-level mathematics to find ways to get their drivers going even faster. Using their special knowledge, racecar mechanics tweak engines, brakes, and suspensions, always searching for some adjustment that can shave even a fraction of a second off the drivers' times.

Go Online to Find Out More!
Test your speed at http:// www.uptoten.com/ kids/kidsgames- mainindex.html.

Rodeo Cowboy

A bull rider flies off the back of his bull during a rodeo. *AP Photo/Shawnee News-Star, Jennifer Pitts*

Lots of little kids go through a cowboy stage—wearing cowboy boots and hats to the grocery store, trying to lasso stuffed animals (or siblings!), and even imagining showdowns at sunset. Most kids, however, grow out of this phase and go on to do other things.

But there are others who grow up to be real cowboys (and cowgirls). Every spring thousands of wannabe cowboys pull on their boots and fix

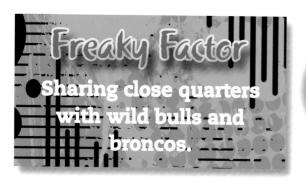

What Do You Think?

Which rodeo stunt do you think would be the hardest to perform? The most dangerous? Which one would you want to learn if only you got the chance?

their hats before saddling up for the rough-and-tumble of the American rodeo circuit. Of course, the things that people now do at rodeos used to be routine chores that cowboys performed at work on a ranch or long ago when settling the wild Wild West. These days, rodeo riding is considered an extreme sport and, like other big-time sports, the competition is best left to the professionals.

Rodeos are held in arenas and usually include at least seven main events. The most standard events are bareback riding, steer wrestling, team roping, saddle bronc, tie-down roping, barrel racing, and bull riding. Almost all of these events pit man (or woman) against beast—whether it's a bucking bronco or an irate bull. In most events, brute strength helps. But it takes skill, good timing, and a lot of luck to make the big bucks in rodeo.

Rodeo cowboys don't have to compete in every event, but they do have to work hard to get really good in at least one event to stay competitive. Work-

WOW!

According to the Professional Rodeo Cowboy Association, as of 2007, the most money a rodeo cowboy had won over an entire career was $2,872,454; the most a cowboy had won in one year was $425,115; and the most a cowboy had won at just one rodeo was $142,644.

GO FOR IT IF...

You are still a cowboy (or cowgirl) at heart.

You're not really into pain. It's rare to get off a bucking bronco without a few bumps and bruises.

FORGET ABOUT IT IF...

ing the rodeo circuit involves a different type of lifestyle. Cowboys must travel around the country to compete in big events. Although there are hundreds of events all over the country, some of the most famous and important ones include Cheyenne Frontier Days in Wyoming, Rodeo Houston in Texas, the Reno Rodeo in Nevada, and National Western Rodeo in Colorado. Unlike their peers in professional football and basketball who play—win or lose—under high-paying contracts, rodeo riders only get paid when they win. Needless to say, this fact gives rodeo cowboys good reason to stay motivated and work hard, but it sometimes keeps them broke, too.

You probably already know this—especially if you've ever seen a cowboy try to ride a bull—but rodeo riding is really dangerous. It's risky enough to bounce around on the back of a wild animal that isn't keen on the idea of giving people "piggyback" rides, but even the best cowboys only manage to hang on for a matter of seconds. Once they fall off, it's cowboy against bull, with only a crazy rodeo clown to distract the bull while the cowboy runs to safety.

Go Online to Find Out More!

Learn about what made cowboys so rough-and-tumble at http://www.thewildwest.org/interface/index.php?action=186.

Tattoo Artist

A tattoo artist works on a man's back.
Stonehill/zefa/Corbis

matter how old the "inked" individual was when he or she got it or even if the tattoo actually said "Mom" on it!

Fast-forward to today and you'll find a completely different scene. Tattoos have gone mainstream! In fact, tattoos are considered by many to be a contemporary art form. Those who decide to have tattoos—and these days it's just as likely to be Mom herself as it is an 18-year-old celebrating a rite of passage or a senior citizen going for the gusto—are likely to encounter pristine, clinic-like conditions in tattoo studios nowadays.

There was a time, not so very long ago, when tattoos were strictly the domain of rough and tough soldiers, sailors, and marines. Oh, and don't forget the motorcycle riders. Tattoos were commonly applied in dingy tattoo parlors and were sure to be met with disapproval from Mom—no

What Do You Think?

Think you've got what it takes to be a tattoo artist? Draw some possible tattoos and start filling up your portfolio to wow customers!

They may choose a design from a wide range of tasteful (or crude, depending on their preferences) stencil designs, or they may ask for (and pay dearly for) an original work of art to be tattooed on the body part of their choice.

Either way, there are many needles involved. Unfortunately, the only way to create a permanent tattoo is to poke needles dipped in ink into the second layer of skin (if it's in the first, it'll just wash off after a bit). Modern tattoo instruments today inject the needle into the skin at 50 to 30,000 times per minute! Ouch! Even though the ink goes in quickly, the process of creating the tattoo can take minutes (if it's an itty-bitty design) or hours (if it's larger). Some of the really difficult ones take months to create!

Just like more traditional artists who create art using brushes and paint, it takes a lot of training and talent to excel in this field. In fact, it takes about five years to become a certified tattooist. Most start out taking drawing classes, and then they work as apprentices in tattoo shops until their mentors believe they're ready to head out and create art. During that time, they learn more about tattoos and creative drawing than most people learn in a lifetime.

Even though tattoos are a particularly "hot" trend these days, tattoos

WOW!

In 1936 *Life* magazine estimated that 10 million, or approximately 6 percent, of Americans had at least one tattoo; in 2003 a Harris Poll found that the number had nearly tripled to include 16 percent; and in 2006 the Pew Research Center found that 36 percent of those ages 18 to 25 and 40 percent of those ages 26 to 40 had at least one tattoo.

GO FOR IT IF. . .

Art is your favorite way
to express yourself.

- - - - - - - - - - - - - - -

You freak out at the
sight of needles.

FORGET ABOUT IT IF. . .

have been around for thousands of years. In the past, many cultures created distinct styles and techniques for tattooing that continue to inspire many of today's artists. Of course, no one does tattoos like the Polynesians of old. For centuries people in faraway places like Samoa and Fiji have considered elaborate, full-body tattoos to be a traditional rite of passage used in their cultures to indicate status in society.

Some people do get carried away and use their entire bodies as canvases for tattooed art. But most are a bit more discrete, opting for smaller designs on ankles, backs, or arms. Many people get hooked, though, and find that one tattoo is simply not enough. It's one of those art forms where there's something for anyone who wants to be a walking work of art.

Go Online to Find Out More!
Find out more than you probably ever wanted to know about tattoos at http:// health.howstuffworks.com/ tattoo.htm.

Taxidermist

A taxidermist works on a stuffed lion in his workshop. *Bloomberg News/Landov*

Picture this: You are at a natural history museum looking at an exhibit of wildlife in their native habitats. There's a jungle scene, a forest scene, a marsh scene, and so on. Everything seems so real that you have to keep reminding yourself that you aren't really on a safari or a camping trip. Look at that grass, those trees, and all that vegetation. And, whoa, the animals... Is it your imagination or did that lion over there just move?

The reason that everything looks so real is because a lot of things—particularly the animals—*are* real. Or at least they were. The lifelike, three-dimensional animals you encounter in places like museums, other types

29

of public areas, and even in some people's homes are the handiwork of taxidermists. Sometimes they use real animals as models and create a replica using a variety of materials including plastic and metal. Other times they actually use the skin and bones of a formerly live (in other words, dead!) animal to make an amazingly realistic model.

In earlier times, taxidermists used crude materials like straw to stuff animal skins. Needless to say, it took a lot of skill (and a little luck!) to make the animals look authentic. These days, the straw has been replaced by clay that taxidermists use with a wide variety of special tools to replicate precise positions and structures in very realistic ways.

This type of animal artistry requires a mix of professional crafting skills that include carpentry, woodworking, tanning, molding, and casting, as well as traditional fine art skills in sculpture, painting, and drawing. Sometimes all these tasks are performed by a single taxidermist, but often a job like this requires teamwork.

Okay, now that you know that taxidermy involves reproducing life-like models of animals, and that

What Do You Think?
How do you think knowing something about animal anatomy would help taxidermists make their work look more realistic?

WOW!

Ever heard of a jackalope? It's a mix between a jackrabbit and an antelope—and it's totally fake! Crypto-taxidermy is the art of creating animals that don't actually exist, from mythical beings like unicorns to extinct species like saber-toothed tigers.

GO FOR IT IF. . .

You like the idea of
mixing nature and art.

- - - - - - - - - - - - - -

You'd rather stick to more
traditional art forms.

FORGET ABOUT IT IF. . .

taxidermists are highly skilled artists, you may well be wondering why
they do what they do—besides creating figures for cool museum exhibits,
that is. Well...go back to that imaginary world again. This time you're
just back from a deep-sea fishing trip
and, wow, have you caught a big one!
What are you going to do with this
prized catch? Eat it? No way! You're
going to take it to a taxidermist and
have them preserve it and mount it
so that everyone who sees it hang-
ing on your wall will know what an
awesome fisher you are. Repeat this
scenario for a hunter who has just
bagged a deer with a very impressive
set of antlers, and for the big game
hunter just back from a jungle safari.

Between supplying sports lovers
like these with "trophies" for their
home mantelpieces and providing
museums and other public places
with realistic educational tools, a
good taxidermist can keep him- or
herself very busy!

Go Online to Find Out More!

**Learn more about the
animal kingdom at http://
www.sheppardsoftware.
com/web_games_trivia_
animal.htm.**

Vermiculturist

Worms get a bad rap. Just because worms have no arms, no legs, and no eyes, people seem to think they're not good for anything but fish bait. So maybe the fact that worms are wiggly, slimy, and sort of ugly has a little

A worm farmer displays some of the livestock from his farm. These worms guzzle scrap food from the tables of a hotel restaurant, quietly doing their bit to save the planet. *Howard Burditt/Reuters/Landov*

something to do with the "Yuck, it's a worm" sentiment. But even so...

It's a good thing that vermiculturists dig a little deeper than most people to uncover a worm's finer points. Here's the thing: Worms are good for a lot of things. In fact, they are good for so many things that vermiculturists, or professional worm farmers, earn their living by farming worms.

Believe it or not, worms are really important to the environment. One

of the things they do best is turn compost piles of human biodegradable waste into a very effective, earth- and human-friendly fertilizer that is used to help all things green grow bigger and better. And how do they do this, you wonder? They eat all the trash and leave nutrient-rich worm castings (otherwise known as worm poop!) behind. Please don't hold this nasty-sounding habit against the poor little critters, because they are just doing their part to keep the cycle of life going around. But, really, who knew that worms were such an important, if unpleasant, part of the world's food chain?

Over time, vermiculturists have experimented with different methods and various worm species to create the best results. Out of the 4,400 different species of worms (including exotic ones like glowworms and silkworms and especially icky ones like tapeworms), guess which one proved itself king of the compost pile? The common, everyday red worm wears that crown! These worms like to burrow into the top layers of compost and eat, eat, eat! And as you well know from personal experience, what goes in must come out!

So what does all this have to do with a vermiculturist's earning a living? Anybody can throw table scraps like old fruit and veggie peels, broken egg shells, coffee grinds, leftover food, tea bags, and even tiny bits of meat on a pile of dirt. However, not everyone wants to scoop up the worm castings, package them in bags, and sell them to commercial farmers and

WOW!

The largest earthworm in the world was found in South Africa, and it was 22 feet long!

GO FOR IT IF...

You love getting down
and dirty!

- - - - - - - - - - - - -

You always insist that
someone else bait your
fishhook when you
go fishing.

FORGET ABOUT IT IF...

backyard gardeners as fertilizer. For
that matter, not everyone wants to

deal with compost piles so massive
that they create tons of worm waste
every year, either. But they do want
the wonderful results of worm-fertil-
ized soil, which is how some vermiculturists worm their way into their
paychecks.

Go Online to Find Out More!

Freak your friends out
with crazy worm facts at
http://yucky.discovery.
com/noflash/worm/
index.html.

More Freaky Jobs

In case you aren't completely freaked out yet, the following are some more, um, rather unusual job choices waiting for those looking for offbeat ways to spend their workdays. And yes, some people really do get paid to wrestle alligators, babysit bees, farm fish, and do other wacky things.

Alligator Wrestler

Rough scales covering its body, beady eyes above the water scoping out prey, ridged tail whipping dangerously from side to side, pointed fangs dripping slime…an image that scary doesn't exactly translate to "Wrestle me!" for most people.

However, nobody ever said that alligator wrestlers were "most people." In fact, there are probably only a few dozen of these wrestlers in the entire United States! Alligator wrestlers capture and subdue alligators as a show for excited audiences.

They don't capture alligators in the wild—they aren't trying to get themselves killed, after all—but the gators they wrestle are more than dangerous enough to frighten the average person.

Alligator wrestlers aren't immune to the pleasures of scaring the wits out of a crowd of people, but they actually do what they do as a way to educate their audiences about the endangered animal. Their goal is to teach people to respect the reptiles, not to freak them out with fear. Even so, most people are still happy to leave the wrestling to the professionals.

Beekeeper

When bees don't pollinate, people don't eat. It seems simple enough… until something goes wrong. For instance, the world is currently experiencing some sort of weird bee epidemic that threatens to wreak havoc on the world's food supplies.

Professional beekeepers, or apiculturists ("apis" is Latin for "bee"), are busy as bees trying to do something about it. They are taking extra precautions to protect their hives (each of which can be home to up to a million bees!) and are looking at ways to keep their bees buzzing around doing what bees are supposed to do: make honey and pollinate crops (and, occasionally, sting a human who dares get in their way!).

Speaking of bee stings...you'll want to know that apiculturists use protective clothing when working with their hives. In fact, they pretty much cover themselves from head to toe in gloves, hats, and veils to keep from being stung.

Fish Farmer

What if you could walk outside your door and find in your backyard ponds thousands of fish splashing around just begging to be caught? Sound like a fishing paradise? Maybe it's the next best thing: It's a fish farm!

Fish farms are places that raise fish commercially, selling them to restaurants, supermarkets, and bait shops. They keep fish in tanks or enclosures and give them plenty of food to make them nice and plump. Fish farmers watch the fish to make sure they're growing correctly, keeping them healthy and happy. They are careful to keep the water pure and fresh, and constantly monitor the amount of oxygen in the water to keep the fish breathing easily.

Fish farms come in all shapes and sizes, as does their "livestock." Just about any type of fish can be farmed, but the most popular ones are salmon, catfish, tilapia, and trout. Some farms even raise shellfish, including lobsters and clams.

Foley Artist

There was a time when movies were absolutely silent. That's sometimes hard to believe with today's thunderous, action-packed films. But even today all of that noise doesn't just end up in a movie naturally. Specially trained film specialists, called Foley artists, actually *put* noise into movies to make them more realistic.

Since movies involve lots of make-believe (action heroes aren't using real guns and aren't actually punching out their opponents in fight scenes), Foley artists work in special sound studios to add noises that make movies sound as believable as they look. These artists use anything from breakable plates and bowling balls to high-tech sound effects to create just the right sounds. When a Foley artist does the job well, the movie sounds so real you'd never guess it wasn't.

Museum Curator

Ever wanted to touch a mummy? See an ancient Chinese silk robe? Put on an African tribal mask? Become a museum curator!

Museum curators work in—you guessed it—museums. They deal with some of the world's most unusual artifacts and collections out there as they create the perfect exhibit for their museum guests. They research the history and significance of these treasures and, if the objects are espe-cially important, they may present lectures or symposiums for interested museum lovers.

But what kinds of things do museum curators actually work with? It depends on the museum. A natural science museum curator may catalogue and arrange tons of insect skeletons, while an art museum cura-tor might focus on beautiful vases or sculptures. Some super-lucky cura-tors even get to work with dinosaur bones!

Obituary Writer

Thanks to obituary writers, dead peo-ple get one last chance to tell their life stories. Newspapers print these stories about the rich and famous as well as those not so rich and famous. The biggest difference is that if you are rich and famous when you die, your death will be considered news-worthy, so newspapers will carry the story for free. If you're not, your loved ones will have to pony up some money to see your name in print.

An obituary provides a summary of a person's life, a task that can be quite a challenge for obituary writers. In some cases, the deceased has done so much and left so much behind that it's hard to get the story down to 250 words or fewer. In other cases, even finding 250 words to write about him or her can require a great deal of creativity. Fortunately, since you're still here reading this, you've got time to make sure to give the person who writes your obituary loads of material to work with!

Plastic Surgeon

Have you ever looked in the mirror and thought, "I wish I had a different nose (or chin or lips...)"? According to the American Society for Aesthetic Plastic Surgery, nearly 11.7 million Americans have done the same thing. The difference is that they actually did something about it by going to a plastic surgeon for some sort of cosmetic procedure. Common plastic surgery procedures include liposuction (to remove unwanted fat from around the waist, hips, thighs, and other places on the body), face-lifts (to smooth out wrinkles), rhinoplasty (otherwise known as "nose

jobs"), and Botox injections (to plump up various parts of the face to give it a more youthful appearance).

Not all of these procedures were due to personal preference or sheer vanity, however. Many of the surgeries were preformed on people who were born with birth defects or who were injured in accidents. In these cases, plastic surgeons repair or reconstruct physical deformities to help people breathe better, walk better, eat better, and improve the overall quality of their lives.

Toilet Paper Manufacturer

There are some jobs that people tend to take for granted, but the reality is if someone didn't do them, we'd all be in trouble. Take toilet paper manufacturers, for instance. Who would have thought that highly intelligent (and in some cases, highly paid) people spend their days making roll after roll of squeezable soft toilet paper? Theirs is a constant quest to find ways to make their product softer, stronger, or more environmentally friendly than the competition's.

And aren't you glad somebody takes the time to care? Without them we might have to revert back to when toilet paper was invented in 14th-century China—but only the emperor could use it! Commoners were on their own to find their personal grooming materials.

So the next time you've "gotta go," give a shout-out for toilet paper manufacturers—for all they do to make the world a better place!

Real People, Freaky Jobs

What do bizarre food, raging bulls, racecars, and worms have in common? They are the main ingredients in the following people's fabulously freaky jobs!

PEOPLE PROFILE #1: Chris Schaefer, Bizarre Food Chef

Did you know that every year you eat around *two pounds* of insects...without even realizing it? In cultures all over the world, though, insects are a typical ingredient used in cooking, and it is no different in Chris Schaefer's kitchen. Schaefer is a chef at Typhoon, a Pan-Asian fusion restaurant in Santa Monica, California, where he mixes Taiwanese stir-fried crickets, Singapore-style scorpions, whole water bugs, and more into his dishes.

With 25 years of cooking experience, Schaefer is a veteran chef, but his career as a master of kooky cookery started when he began to work at Typhoon. Schaefer cooks with more than insects—his restaurant offers about 80 items for hungry diners to choose from—but the menu devotes an entire section to creepy crawly delights. While some people "play it safe" by ordering plates that you might see at your local Chinese spot, Schaefer says that his restaurant serves a ton of customers eager to try even his strangest creations. For them, the weirder, the better!

So, what is the most bizarre dish Schaefer has ever whipped up? Prepare yourself—pig intestine stew. At Halloween time, Schaefer and the other chefs take "bizarre" to another level, adding in various animal body parts—brains, entrails, feet, and so on—and, of course, even more insects. The stew, though, is what Schaefer puts at the top of his list of weird...and he knows weird food!

A last bit of advice from Schaefer: In case you ever have the opportunity to munch on a water bug, "Don't eat the wings!"

PEOPLE PROFILE #2: Luke Snyder, Professional Bull Rider

When it comes to being Luke Snyder, a typical day on the job starts when he "cowboys up"—gets mentally prepared to give it his all—and grabs the bull by the horns...literally! At the tender age of nine, Luke Snyder fell in love with bull riding. He attended a professional rodeo in nearby Kansas City, Missouri, watched every single event, and made a decision: For better or for worse, for richer or for poorer, in sickness and in health, he wanted to be a professional bull rider. Today, he *is* a professional bull rider, and he has certainly lived out those vows during his career.

The very day of his first rodeo, he signed up for youth rodeo school (much like football or baseball camp). In every attempt in the three days of riding steers, he could not stay atop his mount for more than a second. Even though he was not what you'd call a "natural" at bull riding, he loved rodeo school and went home craving more. At 14, Snyder moved up to riding the big bulls that professionals compete with, and on his 18th birthday—note that the *youngest* age you can be a professional bull rider is 18—he entered his first professional bull riding competition. It was a happy birthday, for sure: He finished in third place, went on to grab first place in a competition the following day, and from there was swept off to compete in the Built Ford Tough bull riding series. That year he was the Professional Bull Riders, Inc. World Finals Winner and was honored by them as their Rookie of the Year. He'd come a long way from being tossed off a horse in the blink of an eye, wouldn't you say?

Since his early successes, Snyder has not pulled up on the reigns at all, and he continues to prove himself as a great bull rider. In the 2007 season, he broke the longstanding record for consecutive events participated in by a rider. This record comes as a result of his refusal to sit out at any events, even when he suffered from broken bones in his leg and face and torn ligaments in one of his knees. "In sickness and in health," indeed!

PEOPLE PROFILE #3: Mark Sanderson, Racecar Mechanic

The sound of engines roaring, the sight of headlights flashing against metal, the feel of fingers gripping a steering wheel, the scent of auto exhaust, and the taste of adventure—the job of a racecar mechanic is one that involves all of Mark Sanderson's senses. Sanderson works at Wyotech in Blairsville, Pennsylvania, as an instructor in the High Performance Powertrains concentration of the Automotive Technology department. Translation: He has a really cool job! At the technical school, he provides mechanics-to-be with up-to-date specialty training in lots of high-performance automotive applications. He shares his expertise in order to help his students gain the knowledge they need to become automotive professionals, too.

Sanderson's love of mechanics and automotives began at a very early age; what started out as simple tinkering grew as he worked on various motorcycles and dirt bikes in his teens. After graduating from high school, Sanderson entered the Ford ASSET (Automotive Student Service Educational Training) program, an automotive school hosted by Ford Motor Company, Ford and Lincoln Mercury dealers, and some local community colleges.

Racecar mechanics are certainly not born with their automotive knowledge. Just look at Sanderson: When he entered the Ford ASSET program, he didn't even know how to change the oil in a car! Now he has tons of experience in his field and really enjoys what he does. The "rush" he feels every time he steps onto a racetrack is what he looks forward to, and his passion hasn't faded in all of his years on the job. His words of wisdom are, "Do what you love. If you love cars and love racing, go for it." So, ladies and gentlemen, start your engines!

PEOPLE PROFILE #4: Anna Carter, Vermiculturist

Some say dogs are man's best friend, but worms are the companions of choice for Anna Carter. Now a certified Master Gardener, Carter's long history of working with worms dates back to when she was an adventuresome child living in the Bay Area of California. A tomboy, Carter spent a lot of time playing outdoors. Heavy rain sent the worms wriggling to the surface and up out of the ground. Carter enjoyed playing with the slippery dirt dwellers when they came up to say, "Hello!" And so, a hobby was born.

Her hobby soon became a business, though. She gathered up many of the worms she found and placed them in wooden crates for her family to sell as bait to fishermen. Customers asked to buy the worm castings (meaning worm poop!) to improve their garden soil, and Carter saw that other people were interested in worms, too (though maybe not in the same friendly way!).

She noticed that the soil in her community was unhealthy and could use a boost from nutrient-rich worm castings. After becoming a Master Gardener, she now has a worm castings business—which sells worm poop by the ton!—and she uses her profits for many community efforts, such as building free urban orchards to grow organic food for inner-city members.

Which worm is her favorite, you might be wondering? The California Red Wiggler, because "it has a personality!" In addition to making high-nutrient castings, this worm is self-sufficient and strong. Sounds a lot like Carter...no wonder they're friends!

Freaky Job Playground

You've read about freaky jobs that other people do. Here's your chance to play around with the idea of having a freaky job yourself someday. So what do you think? Could you do it? Would you dare? (Oh, and by the way, if this book doesn't belong to you, please use a separate sheet of paper.)

★ Watch Out, Freaky Job, Here I Come

First, imagine that you're all grown up and ready to tackle a freaky career...

Would You Do It?	Can't Wait to Try It Someday!	Maybe—If I Ever Get The Nerve!	Not A Chance!
Bizarre Food Chef			
Circus Performer			
Cryptologist			
Genetic Engineer			
Pet Psychologist			
Racecar Mechanic			
Rodeo Cowboy			
Tattoo Artist			
Taxidermist			
Vermiculturist			

⬟ Mirror, Mirror on the Wall…

Which of these jobs is the freakiest of all?

- ◎ Alligator Wrestler
- ◎ Beekeeper
- ◎ Fish Farmer
- ◎ Foley Artist
- ◎ Museum Curator
- ◎ Obituary Writer
- ◎ Plastic Surgeon
- ◎ Toilet Paper Manufacturer

⬟ Help Wanted: Person with Unusual Skills for a Freaky Job

Take your pick of the freaky jobs listed above and pretend that you have to hire someone to fill this out-of-the-ordinary job. Quick! Make up a newspaper ad that will get just the right person to respond. Be sure to weed out the wannabes from the real thing by emphasizing the special "talents" it takes to get the job done.

⬟ Hot off the Press!

What's your idea of a totally freaky job? Can you invent one so abso-lutely and totally unusual that people everywhere will scratch their heads in wonder that someone would actually get paid to do it?

Pretend that a news magazine thinks your job is so unique that they want to feature you on its front cover. They ask you to write a short story about what you do. Include lots of behind-the-scenes information, and don't forget to include stories about some of your wildest on-the-job adventures!

⬟ One More Thing…

Here's some room to list any good books or interesting Web sites you find to further explore freaky job ideas. You can use a search engine like http://kids. yahoo.com to search for information by typing in the name of a career you'd like to know more about. You can also ask your school media specialist or librarian for help in finding some books.

Index